UNMOTHERED

A J Akoto

Uncorrected ARC/proof

ARACHNE PRESS

First published in UK 2023 by Arachne Press Limited
100 Grierson Road, London, SE23 1NX
www.arachnepress.com
© A J Akoto 2023

ISBNs
Print: 978-1-913665-80-7 eBook: 978-1-913665-81-4

The moral rights of the author have been asserted.

Cover design *Darkness Follows* © Kevin Threlfall 2023

Printed on woodfree paper by TJ Books, Padstow, England.

Thanks to Muireann Grealy for her proofreading.

The publication of this book is supported using public funding by the National Lottery through Arts Council England.

for Diana,
who told me,
'you will find a way'

UNMOTHERED

Contents

Creatrix

Mothers, first creators,
try to shape us in their own image,
or what they wish they were.

Feel the dip
of finger marks, moulding
muscle and bone like clay.

Our bodies belong not to us
but to the women who

grew us
fed us
know us

enough to end us with a word.

What terror and awe.
And after all, aren't men
afraid of God?

Unborn Ghost

She'd tried for years
to get pregnant again:
this time a daughter.

When, after fifteen years,
she thought it had happened, she fell
on the nearby hill and bled.

Period, miscarriage, whatever it was,
the thought of a child was there.
Someone else was almost here.

I try to take some meaning
from this accident of death,
this overlaying of life on life.

But I know that I'm an accident of fusion
and division, that I've stepped into dead shoes
and that's why life seems to shift away

from my eye line. Every time I snap around
to catch the unborn ghost,
what I've built disintegrates like a bloody wall.

Gorgon

Certain things should be approached
side-on, with a darting gaze,
as you look at a bright goddess
from the corner of your eye.

My mother is a figure ablaze
at the edge of sight; I cannot bear her
head on. I need a sickled blade.
I need a shield, mirror-bright.

Delicacy

You do not have to be a delicacy.
You do not have to be tasty.
You do not have to submit
your body into feminine frailty.
You do not have to ruin your digestion
in an attempt to be digestible.

Your mind can be full
of ice-white rage;
you do not have to be kind.
You do not have to yield
to the pressure to forgive.
Forgiveness does not make you good
and goodness does not require it.

You do not have to exhibit grace,
not in anything.
You do not have to make yourself
a morsel,
not for anyone.

Return of Summer

Bowl of the sky drenched in sun,
everything searing,
smell of fried grass, dust
of cracking trees, air packed.

Somewhere, deep underground,
bodies packed
where no wind can whistle
between them.

A return. Not of last year's summer,
but the sense of those simmering
childhood hours spent reading
under the light of solitude.

Cool relief of those hours free
from the prickle
of her shadow along the wall.

Haunting

foxes stalk　　　　night-murk

ghost flames　　　　swallowing black
　　leap from　　dark　　like blur

like fire-bristled wind　　like shredded
comfort

Unmothered XVI

You spent so long creating
the myth of your good mothering
that you could not live it,
much as a hero boasts loud and long
of his deeds before ever setting foot
outside his door,
and, having talked so much
the time for them has come and gone,
sits down, old and ordinary,
at his table.

Ox-hunger

what is the pulse of fear
a thrumming wire   enlivened
searing   half-angry half-
mystified   unsure which followed
first   what is fear
skin alight   hairs lining up
like wheat burning under
summer   like a bristle of spears
shaking then breaking
splintering in   arrowheads
still sharp and whole
fear
air
wind   field rustling
like an animal's back   like a warrior's
shiver   sensing before he's sensible
of death

***

death   also known as crashing
like a tree   darkness falling
over eyes   never seeing home again
which happens too in life to
the estranged   fearful
of home   whole-heartedly
angry   bonds ossified   bones
muscle
sinew
tissue   carried
to the threshold   across   out
into distance   dead (to you)
while living   measured in miles
rather than realms

***

there is realm of air
there is realm of despair
the very present absence
called hunger   learning young
like chicks swallowing   mother-gorge
how to feed on anger   until
it feeds on you   and then
realm of tasting
realm of wasting   opposite
but cyclical   the midpoints
of air   of despair

***

what is the rhythm of despair   when
men cramped together
in a horse that might burn   settle
into each other's breath   by unison
hypnotise fear
what are the bounds of despair   or
is it borderless   slipping language
      displacing selves
across others   who are selves
Achilles   Patroclus   Achilles   Hector
Achilles   death
all one long map of a man
countries and rivers picked out in scars

***

what is the character of despair   note
who came up with the idea   but
volunteered the duty to others   note
slyness   sucking air out of other
arguments   starving fire with craft

shadowed intent   much like
starvation   feasting
to sickness   disgorging   purging

Cunning

He's a fox. His intelligence is lush,
voluptuous as a circle, snapping shut.
He has sword, he has men —
his bow he left behind to draw him
back — but, more than steel into flesh,
he knows: cunning
can salt a field with dead men
as generously as you'd season meat.

Who Is To Be Saved?

It's a difficult decision,
but all the same, my mother
does what she does best:
saves herself.
Small matter that someone of hers
has to be tossed
in the direction of darkness.
She bets on the flexibility
of childish bones to absorb
the crash, and if not, well,
children's bones heal quickly.

Years later, she comes back,
closing out light behind her.
A shadow crosses my heart,
a spider skitter-scattering
along the muscle of my being.
She's back to save herself,
and this time, needs my help.
Needs my presence. Strange,
because I've always thought myself
an absence. Has she not felt the shape
of me, where I should have been
by her side?

She also needs my darkness.
Did I not mention?
When I landed in the dark,
I stayed there. Yet
she holds out her hand
and I'm hers again. Even when
she recoils at my mangling,
because some bones do not heal,
and some hurts set themselves wrong,
I'm still hers.

Daughterhood

No one had ever told her
the possibility of undaughterhood.
Or how the weight of mothers
can be shrugged off —
not like a coat but
like the rolling stone of a sepulchre,
hard at first, then easier with the inertia,
and then a last flick.

No one had told her that she could be good
and undutiful at the same time.
Oh, she thought, if I ever
have a daughter, I will tell her
that she can be free of me.
Perhaps that way she won't want to be,
but if she does, I'll know
the brightness of having told her
that such a wonder exists.

Mutation (water)

Water of life, blessed water, holy water, water for baptism, water as blood, water as wine, water as libation, water for naming, water for exorcising, water as commemoration, water as bearing, water as birthing, water as rebirth, water as element, water as sphere, water on fire, water falling through air into water, water as drowning, water muffling sense yet magnifying sound, water as pressure, water wearing away, water raging, water saving, water as tears, water for questioning, water as torture, water as maddening, water as dream, water as hallucination, water as thirst, water as cure, water as poison, water for burying, water for dying.

Your Death

Like when a prisoner sees his jailer falter
a foot from the door, hand clenched
around the key even while falling to the floor,

and rejoices, reaches out to grasp his freedom,
but finds that his arm stretching
through the bars is an inch too short.

He is in a worse place than before,
here with the dead alone,
his source of water, food, sustaining anger: gone.

I will come and set my stone before you

Which remains an obscure saying
to me but feels, if not true,
then right.

Escaping Arrangements

Trees, bladed with leaves. The moon as an opening shiver. A name — your name — arrowed along the air behind you. And what now? Hunted by love in its hardest form. Duty is a form of love otherwise you wouldn't do it. What, then, does your refusal mean? The snake that crossed your path in the fractured light of this last morning, flicked its trifurcated tongue at you — what does it mean? The refusal of your patterned scars to raise. The shake that set in when you were not told, but heard, like any stranger passing through might hear. Arrangements have been made. What does it mean, dripped in your mother's and your grandmother's finery? That shake. That ache. Your feet — weighted with gold, digging deeper into the earth than all your prior casual steps added together — have carried you here. To this particular canopy. To the trees that everyone circles rather than walk through. What does it mean that you are waiting beneath daggers of green-fall? A breeze rises and you feel it as a healer's herb-soaked cloth trailing your skin. The leaves swing up in a gust, gathering their momentum. Look up at them, falling now — what does it mean?

Womanhood

Come, let me tell you what womanhood
is, my aunt laughs behind her cracked teeth.
I have done a lot for peace and quiet,
given a lot. The parts of myself
I didn't want to give, I found
myself throwing into rising fights,
to defuse them. The parts I should
have let fly out like feathered needles
through a blow dart, I kept hidden
in the sheath of my heart. They are still
very sharp, but with nowhere to go now,
no one to sink into. I have kept quiet
to keep the peace. Not my peace,
but still, I have been the woman
my mother was, and my grandmother.
Peaceful women. My aunt clicks her tongue
behind her teeth. Don't be, and I can't tell
if it's a command or a plea. Don't be peaceful?
I ask. Don't be a woman, she says.

Under Pressure

She's had a child. Now
everyone can get off her case.

Three years go by,
and, *time to have another?*
people tease.

Five years: this being
she's birthed, pulling love
from her like spider's silk,
thin, translucent thread
with the tensile strength of steel.

Time to have another, everyone
around her says, not asking
and not teasing.

Her husband shrugs. Well it's what you
should do, he says, casual casual,

but she can see the glaze
over his eyes, his anticipated joy
in the 'trying'. Not so much
the raising.

What does your daughter
like to eat? she asks him.
Answer that, she shrugs,
and we can have another.

Candour

For all the times you laughed
without showing teeth
— because they were gritted
behind the smile,
because you did not have
the freedom of candour —

laugh open-mouthed now.

Longing

When I sleep, if I sleep,
the dreamscape is full of longing.
Not mine. Full of pleading
for contact, connection,
something more than silence,
although it may be less than peace.
If you would leave me alone
I would reach out to you,
I tell the longing, and it twists
itself up with my words
until I wonder if it's mine,
if I'm saying one thing that is true
and feeling another thing
which is also true.

It is true that you can miss
the idea of a person. That you can plead
into an abyss that turns out to be
a small dark room with a door
with no handle. In a dream
and in real life, a space changes itself
according to your own sense of smallness.
A small room becomes expansive,
a big room a trap, and that is what
love is like when you can't escape it.

If I sleep and the longing arises,
have I carried it there
or is it meeting me where it can?
Dreams are a gathering place,
after all. Is she meeting me
where she can?

Forewarning

Being someone's mother
won't protect you from them.

She doesn't know that,

not grasping
what she has lost.

She wonders at this love
that feels like a fine blade

levered
under the muscle of her heart.

A knife shucked
into the seam of her closed shell,

ready to prise it apart.

An Unsuspicious Death

The second time my mother died
I was nine. The leaves of the trees
trembled with held water, and my eyes
were dry. She's too shocked
to cry, the aunties said.

What they would have said, if they'd known:
she's shocked that what she wished for
happened, and now she feels powerful,
and ashamed.
Now she carries death.

But I was also there
the first time my mother died.
I knew what was left
was only a trace of her
outlined in a body.

I knew she was finished when she stopped
crying, and the tears held in the lip
of her eye hovered there
and dried. When she stopped
squeezing my hand in return.

So this second time is a strange
nothingness of happening.
The aunties cluck about me, and I want
to tell them they are all hens,
and I am a fox with blood under my claws.

Unmothered III

She was a wanderer of Christianity,
posting between the extremes. From church
to church and Father to pastor, seeking,
not only for her but for me. Something to join us
together, make plain the command
to honour your mother and father.

It didn't work. What had been split
between us couldn't be tethered again.

Mapping is a drawing problem

Where mapping is a drawing problem
odysseys are found. So Odysseus
realised when each time he rolled out
the map, it had shifted: sudden
islands; new pathways shaped
by water; an entire sphere of stars,
swerved to the left; lines flocking
and dispersing like an augury
of birds. And always
                    Ithaca
in the same spot, on the other side
of journeys repeated, but never the same.

Unmothered IV

All this time I can't take back,
I should have been your daughter.
I'm lost because I didn't constellate
the blunt star of your fist
with your belief that it was
the bang of a kiss.

Falling Point

Flash of stairs up to falling point. Blood like dark
sheet metal, enough to turn air to tang
but not enough to pull all her iron to a charge
and raise her, disturb the distance
which states that when we fall we die.

A Visitation

Mind brings things in the night.
Dreams, feral-filled
with animals that are not
animals but people:
a red fox, jaw wild,
leaping into the form of a man.

Sweat-infested bed
and a fever of strange acts.

Fear clawing into flesh,
burrowing under
skin. Stinging things.
Spider's fangs pushing in,
scorpion's back arched into its tail,
fox digging in with teeth.

Visitation of old ghosts
in a new dark.

The Word

Memory is a thing bone-bright
behind a locked door. It is hair
that grows dead, and so remains
long after muscle and skin.

It is the book in shrunken hands
whose spine cannot bear opening.
It is the word. And can this bring you
back? Not from the dead. To me?

Unmothered XV

I have a grief to pick at,
like a scab I should let alone
but can't help sliding a nail
under, prising until it lifts off
and the new-skin fibres underneath
stand up like hairs.

The hairs on the back of my neck,
back of my arms, rise
when her absence gains fullness
and I think I see her
slip again into this world.

Knowing she can't be there,
and if she is, by now
she's ghosted
down to bone,
still, I turn.

Nekia

Her.
      Her ghost.

The tree, leafless,
beaded with rain.

Not a drop of gold
among the dark wetness.

Water from summer, green-
scented. A blood-dripped

dip in the earth.
Call her up,

for questioning.
Her, or her ghost.

Doesn't matter
which. As long as

my mother
      answers.

Myth

I have made fortune fear me;
I sweep fate away with my fisted hand.

This is the myth (lie) that makes
and remakes every pain in you. Grandmother,
and aunts too (or perhaps
it's only my mother seething).

Each fate you tried to fight
fills in the edges of your spirit
with resentments major,
resentments minor.

Because I have refused it,
it cannot come to pass.

Which is like saying
you don't believe in ghosts
while the bedsheets shift
themselves in a windowless room.

Yet you also tell histories (stories)
of prophecies (dreams),
and warnings (sharp as truth).

Which house collapsed in a flood
(the ancestral home, of course),
and who died when, in which omen-
filled way (death is never just death).

Magnificent story-teller.
Perhaps that is your fate — using myth
to make and unmake yourself,
reshape family history (misfortune) —

although I won't tell you that
in case it gives you another gift
to battle. Like you, I am
a woman of this family.

What myths, then,
am I making?

I will come and set my stone before you

Which is the long way
of saying I told
you so.

Classic

Orpheus looked back too early
and Aeneas far too late.
Lot's unnamed woman

turned back – 'I want to see'–
and became a pillar of salt.

All these wives,
never quite making it out with their lives.

Abystitus' Ghost

And were you satisfied?

At the end of it all:
blood, unfurled from your womb
and your hands
and your love,
fire-red —

enough to set a bride ablaze —
enough to crumble
a house – wood – lineage –
from under you —

was it enough?

Was the air strong enough
were you light with revenge
were you light with death
were you light with making a man
and breaking that man —

giddy, giddy power —

enough to escape
the tug of the always swelling sea
roaring for revenge?

Unmothered II

There's not much tenderness
in my mother's love.

That's not to say it isn't love,
or that it isn't there,

but that it's fierce and unyielding,
even to me.

Seedings

'Don't forget that I seeded
the groaning earth
with dragons' teeth.

We sail on waves
that break with my brother's
blood.'

This is how I bound him to me
with more than my body,

so that one day, when my stomach
was slack — he having seeded his sons —
he would not leave me.

He left anyway. She was
young and beautiful
and apparently was going to save his life.

He forgot — did he?
He absolved himself of remembering —

that the black waves follow me,
for saving his life,
with breaks of a boy's blood.

Family Business

Her hand, trailing the sea
black as pearl, salt heavy
in her black hair, eyes heavy — grief?
love? she can barely
tell them apart —

as the ship carries her to what
she already suspects is further grief.

But first, more family business.

She hopes, one witch to another,
that her aunt, used
to doing terrible things as she is,
won't revile her –

which she does, as soon as she claps
her palms together at the sight
of her niece.

Her new husband
doesn't recognise it — though she has
a snarling dread
that he doesn't understand women
at all, let alone her — but she knows
the hollow snap of air, as if
her aunt is acknowledging a demon.

Which is fair, considering it all.

And she might have been clapping her hands
At the sight of him.

Protector

She didn't hate her children.
Neither did you.
(Yes, I have to say it, or else
people will think otherwise.)
Only knew how to be fierce, warrior-
subtle. Which is to say, a sword
in each hand and teeth bared.
This was you too.
Her children saw her back as a shield.
Whenever she turned to face them:
well, a sword in both hands
and a glare.
            Only you
would have recognised
her weariness.

A Test of Water

The sea is full of metal (this is bad).
The sea sings over our oars (this too is bad).
The passage of our boat is uncertain.

What is certain: I should have told my daughter
beforehand why she shouldn't listen to the song.
That metal so light and strong in the sea
isn't just strange, but wrong.

That things that sing to you are dangerous.
I used to sing to her.
But I've told her none of this. She dips

a hand in the water, quick.
When she snatches it back, her fingers
are silver. They lift like air
to point over my shoulder.

I look back. See nothing.
Feel nothing, except the terror
of being her mother.
I turn again to face her — gone.

The water, for all its singing,
took her silently.

I drop my oar, search hard until I see
a hand trying to break free, trapped
by the water's surface.

I plunge my hands in, pull
until my arms are full of her
as she tumbles back into the boat,

transformed. So light she feels

like a baby in my gleaming hands.
So beautiful that now I'm afraid
of her. As, I'll come to find,
I'm right to be.

Before her hand picks up the knife

Before her hand picks up the knife,
she digs her fingers into her brow,
trying to grasp how much sharper

she is than the blade.
How little she's been able
to soften. But

in my dreams I am soft,
she says. In my dreams
I am a gentle mother.

In false visions
I have left all my fierceness
behind in my marital bed

and skim the waters,
wine-dark but unbloodied.

The stars pillow my head.
The seas pull my dreams under instead.

Let my ferocity…falter.
This hesitation is a scream,
she says.

Water scoops the words
from her mouth
and salt abrades her tongue.

Her shoulders slump.
It may be relief.
It may be resignation.

I know too much,
not just of witchcraft but
of motherhood,

she says. That's the problem.
What you birth
strangles its way back to you.

I've hurt too many, she says.
Yet stay my hand from
my children, she begs.

The fist of her hand is the size
of her heart, but steady
as it seizes the knife.

Justifications

They are not just my children.
They are their father, reaching

into the future, grasping for a way to extend
himself.

I'll cut him off —

Exception

He looks up at this furious wife,
more witch than wife,
more witch than woman.

Witch-mother, escaping
alive and avenged,
and it's her will that's driven it.

She looks down and smiles
at the absurdity of the man who thought
the name of wife could contain or consume her power.

I will come and set my stone before you

I don't think
she meant this stone though,
weighing down the settled earth above her.

Unmothered XVIII

I think of all the things I want to say
as these three months, a school term, tick down
and her dying unspools into permanence.

How she tried to make me hard
but failed.
How I'm so used to her violence
that kindness opens me like a knife.
How a litany of small destructions has become my tended fire,
yet I wish for light enough to tell the darkness by.

How there will be nothing for either of us
in her final breath, and that it's hopeless,
this attempt to bring us together
when she's moving swiftly away, apart.

I cannot say any of this to a dying woman,
who wants to rage and not be raged at,
wants her life's wrongs
diminished as she diminishes too.

Pain, then morphine, come like gifts,
making time and place fragment.
But admissions come out like stars, including, malice-bright,
that if she could make time leap, she'd jump
back with it over the ditch of my birth.

Stitch

There is breaking.
There is healing.
There is the fissure
in between, like skin
opened by a knife.
You must
stitch yourself back
together.

Archaeologist

...by which measure, she said,
unbury your wrongs; things noticed,
turned in hands and examined,
can be redeemed...

Estrangement

Let us call into question the edges
of our estrangement.

I map it here,
thin contour lines patterning
this ridge of scarring,
that raised knuckle of hurt.

You chart it across the way
where love and fierceness meet,
neither with grace,
neither giving way.

Both of us have etched deep

markings where we've been wronged,
but I do not know where the borders
of your anger are,
as you do not know mine.

I sometimes sense they overlap,
feel the shudder of their crossing,
as lines unpicked inch by inch
and stitch by stitch
draw close again, as if to weave together.

This being the case,
our estrangement is more a reaching
for each other, than a pulling apart.

Violence

I need not
        be violent to myself

I can grip
        deep days
        of affection
as tightly as I hold the days
when her

                fury

at not having made
different decisions
        — including love
        men
        me —
spilled over

when the hard parts
of the day were the
        close-packed

        silences

        in between
        outbursts

bracing
yourself is more exhausting than the frightening
        clarity of pain

      these days,
when I brace myself and the pain
doesn't come

I remember the particular
violence of the anticipation
        of violence

how I am still re-enacting it
but in fact need no longer
        be violent to myself

Why don't you want children?

Because I know I'd likely fail the test —
the one where you'd give your life
for your child's sake — and though everyone says
that changes once they're in your arms,
mine wouldn't stand a chance.
The truth of that gathers like an ache.

I know it from the other side, that place
where there's no steering of the fearful gap
between mother and child.
I'd fail, looking at their trusting face,
and never reach the line that marks
not fucking up so terribly
that it can't be reconciled.

Unmothered XIX

'Do you…
              hate her?'

'No. And
that's
the difficulty.'

Day Dawns Dark

And here I am, lost
in a thick wood, the path
through shifting to the left
of my feet with every step,
so that I'm never on it.
The ground is knotted
and my fear is knotted
around my neck. And if
I were to manage speech,
it would not be God
I called out for, but
someone very human
and far more dangerous
to me. Dangerous
enough to find me,
perhaps to save me,
as only mothers can.

Unmothered I

Perhaps if I had tried a little harder to fail in some
things,
I would have failed in anger too.
But your anger taught me too well to succeed in
everything,
including silence.